# MENTORED BY FAILURE

A 5-Point Guide to Long-Term Success in the Beauty & Style Industry

*by* TYE CALDWELL

CALDWELL PUBLISHING
MCKINNEY, TEXAS

Mentored by Failure: A 5-Point Guide to Long-Term Success in
the Beauty & Style Industry
by TYE CALDWELL

Printed in the United States of America.

ISBN: 1519100906
ISBN-13: 978-1-51910-090-0

*edited by* COURTNEY CALDWELL
*interior pages designed by* JOHNNY MACK & CALDWELL PUBLISHING
*cover design and photography by* AIR DESIGNS

To order additional copies of this resource, write
Caldwell Publishing
PO Box 2933
McKinney, TX 75070;
email courtney@salon74bytye.com;
order online at www.salon74bytye.com;
order online at amazon.com

## What are people saying about MENTORED BY FAILURE?

*Mentored By Failure* speaks to the business owner that has to be detailed, relationship-focused, and consistent. In a world that is so visual, you have to bring your "A" game everyday to the beauty industry. But this book really speaks to us all if we're willing to take this simple, practical, but powerful message into our everyday lives. Tye is a man of character, and has developed a plan and strategy that works. The principles in this book can take you on the road less traveled if you're willing to apply them to your business and life.

Mike Singletary
Pro Football Hall of Fame
Former Head Coach of the San Francisco 49ers

Tye's journey as an entrepreneur will inspire and energize all who have—till this very moment—chosen to sit on the sideline of forging their own destiny. It is not only a perfect prescription for how to reach success in an established industry, but a blueprint on how to survive, strive, and thrive when confronted by adversity. *Mentored by Failure* is a clarion call of action to rise above mediocrity and redefine the future.

T.D. Lowe
Founder & CEO
EnovationNation
Featured in *The Wall Street Journal*, *Washington Post*
2013 Global Hot 100, World Summit on Innovation &
Entrepreneurship

Tye focused on his destiny and not his distractions. After failing his way to success, he is a proud salon entrepreneur with a laundry list of accomplishments. His first book, *Mentored By Failure*, is a five-point guide not only for professionals in the beauty and barber industry, but is a guide for any entrepreneur ready to propel towards success. Learn from someone who has walked in your shoes. These pages are valuable lessons that act as an invaluable resource to your personal, professional, and financial life.

Les Brown
World's Leading Motivational Speaker
International Speaker-Trainer & Coach
Author of *Live Your Best Life*

Success does not come overnight. More often than not, it comes from learning through direct exposure. The beauty of this insightful, must-read book is that you can learn from Tye's experiences to place yourself strategically on the road to success. Take the time to truly learn from those who have gone before you. Then take the time to read every page of *Mentored by Failure* to start and/or relaunch your own business.

Donishea Martinez
Regional Sales Director
Genentech

In a world where many allow their dreams and goals to be thwarted by past missteps, *Mentored by Failure* shows that if we allow God to work, He can use our past failures to guide us towards a bright future. What a unique, well-timed, and culturally-appropriate book we can use to drive individuals to success!

Dr. Conway Edwards
Author of *Leading a Turnaround Ministry: A Process for Exponential Growth*
Pastor, One Community Church
Plano, Texas

Tye has succinctly and experientially exhaled "help" in writing his freshman book, *Mentored by Failure*. I have personally observed and experienced his business acumen and consistent professionalism as a client of Salon74 by Tye. This book is a game-changer, as is he, for all inspiring entrepreneurs driven to succeed in *any* business. It's a compass providing direction from the wisdom gained through Tye's own missteps and lessons learned. He is the Quintessential Mentor for all new barbers and cosmetologists. This book is an invaluable tool; I highly recommend and endorse Tye Caldwell and this must-have guide!

Roland Sigler III, D.D. (Hon.), CDK,
Founder
Butler And Maid Ministries, Inc.

## *Industry Stats & Facts*

The global beauty market is worth an estimated **$265 billion USD**. (That's *billion* with a B.)
Source: http://tinyurl.com/a3lhrol

In 2012, U.S. barbers, hairdressers, and cosmetologists held about 856,200 jobs. **Nearly half were self-employed.**
Source: http://www.nationalbarberboards.com

The number of U.S. industry operators (cosmetologists) is expected to grow at an average annual rate of 5.5%, reaching **1.3 million operators by 2019.**
Source: http://tinyurl.com/a3lhrol

Overall employment of barbers, hairdressers, and cosmetologists is projected to **grow 13 percent** from 2012 to 2022:
Source: http://www.sbdcnet.org/small-business-research-reports/beauty-salon-2014

The **10 best U.S. markets for cosmetologists**: Louisville, Minneapolis, Charleston, San Diego, Dallas, Los Angeles, Salt Lake City, San Francisco, Miami, New York City.
Source: http://www.totalbeauty.com/content/gallery/p-vain-cities/p42672/page10

*This book is dedicated to my best friend and wife, Courtney, who encouraged me to cross the writing finish line, and to my parents, Houston and Zera, who instilled in me "homegrown" professionalism at a young age.*

*To my family, spiritual mothers, friends, and mentors: I love you all and thank each and every one of you for your unremitting support and encouragement along the way.*

# *Contents*

## *Acknowledgments*

Faithful is He who calls you, and He will also bring it to pass. (NASB)
1 Thessalonians 5:24

Without the seed planted in my spirit and the journey I've experienced along the way, this book certainly would not exist. I give all my thanks to God for entrusting me with the delivery of this message and for surrounding me with a strong network of supporters.

I've shared my vision for helping the next generation that will come after me with those who really believe in what I have to offer. These people have given me hope when I questioned myself and encouragement that has pushed me beyond my own expectations.

I am forever indebted to my spiritual mothers and fathers: Ms. Jerri, Ms. Johnetta, Apostle M.E. Johnson, Jr., Elder Sigler, and others who have spoken truth and helped to build my faith along the way.

To my younger brother, Calvin Caldwell, thank you for enthusiastically believing in and supporting this book from the moment you learned of it. An extended thanks to my family, brothers and sisters, Allyson Rhodes, my talented graphics designer, and to Mrs. Bettye Blount, my accountant. You are forever in my prayers.

Finally, I am deeply thankful for my great good fortune to be married to Courtney Dion. The ultimate definition of success in life is that your spouse likes and respects you ever more as the months and years go by. She is not only my most helpful editor-in-residence but also my deepest and most enduring support. Thank you every day for your selflessness, my love.

## *Foreword*

Tye Caldwell should have given up when he started. After being highly regarded as a student-teacher in barber and beauty school and graduating early from an intensive program, he anticipated a lucrative career. But on Tye's first day behind the chair, he worked a 12-hour shift and had only one paying customer.

Beyond the embarrassing looks from his colleagues, the lint in his pocket along with the crinkled ten-dollar bill from his golden client, Tye should have been crushed, heartbroken, discouraged . . . and as you might imagine, he was. He asked himself, "Am I part of the 80% of beauty school graduates that will have to consider another profession?" But Tye was stubborn enough to come back the next day with his head held high and a sense of excitement again and again.

Soon, customers came . . .

Soon, the same customer came a week later and brought a friend . . .

Soon, the same customer came, with the friend, and a cousin . . . and all of a sudden, Tye was a bona fide beauty and barber professional, with a growing, sharp-looking clientele and promising future.

*Mentored By Failure* is a five-point guide not only for professionals in the beauty and barber industry, but this book is a guide for any entrepreneur ready to propel towards success.

Tye focused on the possibilities. How can anyone keep hope alive with just one customer in a 12-hour day? There's not one simple answer.

But Tye did not get discouraged . . .

He teaches us that dreams really do work if you work them . . .

Tye says, focus is everything . . .

Tye says, if you are clear on your vision and remain resilient, your dreams will become a reality . . .

*Mentored By Failure* will save you time and missteps as a professional in any field. Within these pages are valuable lessons that act as an invaluable resource to your personal, professional, and financial life.

Tye focused on his destiny and not his distractions. After failing his way to success, Tye Caldwell is a proud salon entrepreneur with a laundry list of accomplishments. Learn from someone who has walked in your shoes. Let Tye help you take your career to the next level.

Remember, if you do not go after what you want, you'll never have it. If you do not step forward, you'll always be in the same place. Failure is never final! Leap and grow your wings on the way down.

Mamie Brown's Baby Boy,
Les Brown
www.lesbrown.com

## *Preface*

# Your go-forward success depends on your professionalism, *not* your skill set.

I finished school as a Class A barber stylist; in fact, my teachers lauded me as a gifted individual who was sure to have a long, successful career ahead of him. And yet, I don't recall an achievement roadmap being part of the graduation package when I came out of Texas Barber & Beauty College back in the early 90s. In fact, I had a certain uneasy feeling that if I was to succeed, I was going to have to learn fast from one of life's greatest teachers— experience.

In this book I pull from my personal journey—many wins and quite a few losses—that make up the five points that I feel are the basis to a long and successful career.

My goal is to debunk some myths and help lay solid groundwork for the new, young stylists of today and tomorrow. I am not, nor have I ever tried, to recreate the wheel. Like any profession, you will continually need to learn and be open to new ideas, broaden your people skills, and be focused on creating a lifestyle doing what you love. Along with a few tell-tale stories, I offer truth and wisdom to those who are coming after me about how to survive and truly thrive in this industry.

I have to say that after being in this business for more than twenty years, it saddens me to see the integrity of this position slip to a negative placement in people's minds. We are losing so many gifted and talented individuals in this field after just 2-5 short years because of our lack of mentors and understanding how to operate in excellence.

This is the book I would have wanted when I graduated from barber and beauty college decades ago. Others say that it represents a very comprehensive guide to winning in the beauty and style industry. From one stylist to another, I firmly believe that the advice in these chapters will take you to a higher level within your profession if you consistently practice what I recommend.

That I promise.

I hope you find much value in these pages and will commit to applying what you learn. Please drop me a note and let me know which lessons work best for you and which do not. I appreciate your feedback in advance. Know that you are well on your way to long-term success!

— Tye Caldwell
tye@salon74bytye.com

Whether you're lining up a 55-yard field goal, starting a new business, or preparing to pivot in your life or career, it's natural to be afraid of failure. The key is to ensure that your fear of failure is in proportion with the odds of the worst-case scenario actually happening. Focus on preparing for success.

Shawn Achor

Harvard-trained researcher and author of

*Before Happiness*

## *Introduction*

# It's not really about the hair.
Tabitha Coffey

There are several truths about this industry that I've come to learn over the years:

1. This career is not for everyone.

2. The money you earn is not your money.

3. Your professionalism and consistency (NOT your skill set) will determine your go-forward success.

4. If you are disciplined and have a strong work ethic, you will not need a secondary income to survive financially.

5. Essentially you are your own boss, regardless of where you work. *You* are responsible for *you*.

6. This is a career choice where you can truly change lives.

I don't think I've gone a day without someone asking me how I've managed to maintain success in this industry. And with only 20% of beauty school graduates continuing in the field after five short years, I can understand why. I often tell them that it's no different from working in corporate America, but that it takes more grit because you are working for yourself. You have to have the discipline to do the things that most corporate jobs already have in place for you, like find and fund your own health insurance, life insurance, retirement savings, and other benefits that provide some semblance of security. At the end of the day and as Tabitha Coffey says, "It's not really about the hair."

In this book, I pretty much give you the answers to the test. I've also provided notes pages at the end of every chapter so that you can jot down thoughts and reflections along the way.

So if long-term success in the beauty and style industry is your goal, you've picked up the right book. You'll find in the pages that follow:

- Subject-matter expertise from a master stylist and business owner that cannot be found in beauty school textbooks
- A proven framework
- Valuable tips from a 20-year veteran
- Five practical points to set you up for success

Are you ready? Let's begin.

POINT #1

## *Be Focused.*

# Dreams really do work.

John Paul Dejoria

The numbers are truly dismal: only 20% of beauty school graduates continue in this field after only five short years. What accounts for such a high turnover?

Lack of focus.

Early in my career, I learned to keep the main things the main things, yet I have given so much of myself to become successful, maintain professionalism, and remain consistent. Because I've experienced it more times than I'd like to admit, know that it is easy to give up and call it quits when things are not going the way you anticipated. It takes true focus to get to where you want to go. You have to be laser-light focused and stubbornly resilient if you believe in your vision and dreams.

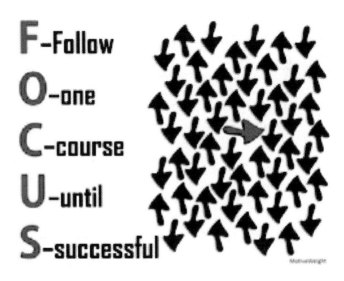

**F**-Follow
**O**-one
**C**-course
**U**-until
**S**-successful

I would have never gotten this far in my career if I had lost focus and quit at every turn. And believe me, it would have been easy to do just that. But failures, setbacks, and disappointments are all going to happen because life is just life: it will test your willpower to persevere.

Here's what I've learned about focus that I'd like to pay forward:

## Always be learning

Like everything else in this world, change is inevitable. And you have to know when and how to change with it. A wise man once said that you are only as smart as the last two books you read. If you can't remember the last couple of titles you consumed (this one doesn't count), then it's probably time for a visit to the local library. Pick up a book on leadership or the psychology of people and get in the habit of learning something new.

| Recommended Reading: Books | Recommended Reading: Magazines |
| --- | --- |
| The Hard Thing About Hard Things: Building a Business When There Are No Easy Answers by Ben Horowitz | Success |
| Talent Is Overrated: What Really Separates World-Class Performers from Everybody Else by Geoffrey Colvin | Entrepreneur |
| Reposition Yourself: Living Life Without Limits by T.D. Jakes | Men's Health or Women's Health |
| Think & Grow Rich by Napoleon Hill | American Salon |

Keep up with changes in client styles and trends but also as it relates to the laws that govern the barber and beauty industry. Were you aware that you no longer have to renew licenses for shampoo techs? How soon after the law passed did you learn about the new mini-salon regulations? By taking continuing education courses and reading fashion magazines, you can stay ahead of regulatory news and cutting-edge trends. Most people look to television shows and TV ads for trend cues. I challenge you to instead travel outside of your city, your state, your country, to get a true feel for other developing beauty and fashion trends.

Exposure and focus in this area is so important if you wish to succeed; it gives you that extra "oomph" to be innovative and really move things forward.

## *Exposure and focus give you a competitive advantage.*

It's not always easy, but I try to keep my pulse on industry and style changes even from behind the chair. In order to run a successful business consistently, you have to plan to work hard because that is definitely what it takes. In addition to learning all you can about your business, marketing, sales, people management, and growth expansion are all important areas in which to invest your time and energy. When I think back, working and managing the salon I worked at prior to starting my own establishment was the single most motivating factor simply because I was able to see past the actual manual work that I was doing and focus more on the business aspect. It was from this unique vantage point—working as a contractor but preparing for the next step—that I really learned to appreciate the value of customer service. What I learned them I put into practice to this very day: no matter how big or small, each individual customer is the reason for my business's growth and success.

Be sure to focus on quality over quantity. The customer is your loudest word-of-mouth advertiser. He or she can either bring people to your establishment or deter others from your business altogether. Remember that each client that gets out of your chair serves as a walking, talking billboard evangelizing their unique experience with others, whether good or bad.

As you learn, know that mistakes will happen and that's ok. <u>Don't avoid making mistakes</u>, because that's how you grow. I have made countless mistakes in my 20+ years in the industry. However, because of those mistakes, I have made great strides, gained a wealth of knowledge, and attained great success. When you stop learning, you stop growing.

## *My best advice: fail* **fast.**

### <u>Believe in yourself and never give up</u>

Focus also requires believing in yourself. If you've never written down your goals, take five minutes to do that now. Don't just rattle them off in your head…find a piece of paper and actually **WRITE THEM DOWN**. Or better yet, do it in the space below. By getting your dreams out of your head and onto your goals list, they become real. And in seeing your goals in written form, you may find that you're closer than you think to your dream.

My career goals:

_____

_____

_____

My financial goals:

_____

_____

_____

My spiritual goals:

_____

_____

_____

My physical goals:

_____

_____

_____

My intellectual goals:

_____

_____

_____

My social goals:

_____

_____

_____

## *When you write down goals that are specific and measurable, they start to breathe on their own.*

As you work to realize your dream, continue to revisit your goals frequently! There will be naysayers and dream killers that will try to squash your vision. But the best thing about dream killers is that if you focus in and use them as motivation, you will not only surprise them and gain their respect, but you will elevate your own self-confidence as well. Get out of your heart and into your head and turn all negatives into positives. <u>Remember: if you can *see* your dream, you can undoubtedly achieve it.</u> If you are surrounded with naysaying family and friends that do not support your dream, find other people who are intelligent risk takers, positive in their reality, and taking steps to achieve their dreams. Dream killers will only block your focus and attack your confidence, so live in your head (be logical) and get out of your emotions when this happens. You will need vision for what you are trying to achieve because small issues will become big issues if you don't handle them well. Believe in yourself and your goals!

<u>Patience is not only a virtue. It will also get you past the starting gate</u>

Patience is a definite requirement in this field because like in life, anything worth having requires diligence and hard work. There is no reason to quit because things aren't happening fast enough. Prime example: my first day on the job after graduating from barber and cosmetology school, I sat in my chair for *twelve hours* and cut **one head.** If anyone should have been worried about how they were going to pay the bills, it should have been me! But I'm here to tell you that if you have the heart, the grit, and the work ethic to build up a solid clientele, the money will follow. You just have to be patient and invest in those things that will make a difference in the long-term.

### *Work the dream, and dream about your work.*

Research shows that only 2 out of 10 graduates stay in the barber and beauty industry after five short years, and I think I know the reason why: **lack of patience.** I see it happen every day: a new stylist starts out excited about the possibilities. Then week one passes and they only service four clients. Week two passes and they only service six clients. Week three passes and the stylist only sees ten people. By the time week four comes around, they're so discouraged that they're already looking to pursue other interests! Look . . . I love what I do and could not imagine doing anything else outside of servicing clients and coaching and mentoring other industry professionals. When you have a dream, be patient and work the vision.

Remember that whatever you feed will live and whatever you starve will die.

Mentors help you see the forest for the trees

Partner with an experienced mentor who meets your definition of success. Seek out someone who has gone before you who will be brutally honest and give you real wisdom on how to make it in this industry. If you can't readily identify a mentor, be sure to read journals and ask other successful professionals in the industry for advice. Put together a network of people that you consider your career "Focus Group." This focus group is made up of people who understand you and your goals, people who will cheer you on when naysayers give you their unsolicited opinion. Believe me, you'll lean on this group often because they have gone through some of the same challenges and come out on the other side. Their help and guidance will be invaluable to your growth.

## *Mentors + focus help get the job done.*

Get focused and stay there

Regardless of what you wanted to be when you grew up, we all strive to attain the "American Dream." Believe it or not, whatever that dream is is in reach for any and every one of us. It just requires more sacrifice than most are willing to give. When it comes to success, there is no such thing as instant gratification; the basics to realizing your BHAG goals (big. hairy. audacious. goals) have not changed or gone out of style. For starters, get clear on your ideal of success and what that looks like to you. Think for 90 seconds and ask yourself how you define your own "American Dream."

## *If you want that dream job,*
## *YOU must create it!*

I am so amazed by the opportunities that are available to us today but equally amazed by our inability to take advantage of them. That is why I firmly believe in being laser-light focused on your goals. Take those calculated risks, have a plan before you leap, and seek out a great mentor who will encourage you when the chips are down.

These are small steps to greatness that one must do everyday. Take it from me…if you are committed and consistent, *they work.*

# NOTES

# NOTES

## POINT #2

### *Be Professional.*

Being a professional is doing the things you love to do, on the days you don't feel like doing them.

Julius Irving

What standards do you live by? What principles guide how you tackle challenges or deal with an unsatisfied customer? If you can't answer that question, start developing some basic guidelines. Remember that this career you've chosen is no different from any other profession. One of the great things about it is that the opportunities are truly endless, but it will take hard work—more than you know but well worth it—as you start to build your career. Be sure to take your job seriously and strive to be the best at what you do. The person you're competing with when you service your clients is *you*, so set a standard of excellence for yourself and your customers.

Would you consider yourself a professional? Do you do the things you love to do on the days you don't feel like doing them? If we want to get technical, *professionalism* is defined as "exhibiting a courteous, conscientious, and generally business-like manner in the workplace" (dictionary.com). Do you operate your business this way? Or do you think your talent makes up for a lack of business etiquette in the workplace? Let me be the first to tell you: It can't. If you are a talented barber or a highly-skilled hair stylist but lack professional courtesy, your career will only go so far. Although there is no one definition on how to be professional, there are multiple elements that work to attract clients and keep them coming back for more. I want to share what I consider to be five must-have traits that can take you from novice to professional if you put them to work consistently:

1. Satisfy the customer with every engagement

To me, this element is the most important because it will become the cornerstone of your success. Without the customer, you just have a hobby. I learned early in my career that it will always cost you less to keep an existing customer satisfied than go out and find a new one. Every client is a potential repeat customer, and that first experience will determine if a repeat will happen. If you treat that customer with poor service, there is a strong possibility that they will not return. Repeat customers is actually a good metric for gauging how your business is doing. If you are providing a great customer experience and leading with professionalism, then that repeat number will be high.

*It always costs less to keep an existing customer happy than to spend time finding a new one.*

Case in point: A longtime client of mine named Steve says that he respects my talent and gift but that alone doesn't keep him coming back for a haircut. Steve says the one thing that makes a difference is my professionalism, my consistency, and the customer experience I provide to every client.

Take a minute to think about yourself as a consumer. In your opinion, which brands get the customer experience right and keep you engaged?

1.

2.

3.

4.

5.

## 2. Be reliable and do what you say

To build a great portfolio of clients requires integrity. Customers should be able to trust you and know that you are going to stand by your word. If you are consistently late to appointments, for example, your reputation for being honest is in jeopardy. And that will bleed over into how much a client will trust you to perform a service.

In the beauty and style industry, time management is often taken for granted. It's not always the stylist's fault, but that doesn't negate the fact that timeliness is the "Holy Grail" for customers. You as the stylist can distance yourself from the competition with that one factor alone. Be reliable and considerate of your client's time because it can truly make or break the relationship. It's okay to over-communicate in this instance. Keep your clients well informed and let them know if anything will cause you to be tardy or miss an appointment.

# *Being on time is the "Holy Grail" for customers in the beauty and style industry.*

3. Communicate effectively and often

Communication is key to building a great relationship. I always make sure that I am thorough when listening to clients' needs and even more thorough when providing feedback. And this is done even before I provide any services to the customer. Remember that listening is primary when your client sits down in your chair. They should have your full attention until their service is complete. Listening and repeating back serve as important process steps to understanding and fulfilling the customers' needs.

Even after the client is out of your chair, there are several options available for continuous customer communications:

## WEB

Web page updates and additions, posting of awards, etc.

Regular email contact, (i.e., electronic newsletter, special promotions, etc.)

## PRINT

Holiday or thank-you cards

Brochures for new services

Poster or marquee advertisements

## PHONE

Calls or text messages just to "stay in touch"

## EVENTS

Customer appreciation events

Grand re-opening celebration

Annual toy and food drive

4. Be pleasant and polite

It costs nothing to smile, yet it can return unbelievable dividends. Being pleasant and polite means so much in today's world of hustle and bustle. As a veteran entrepreneur and working professional in the industry, I have had my share of chaotic moments, but that does not give me permission to have a bad attitude or subject my customers to unprofessional behavior.

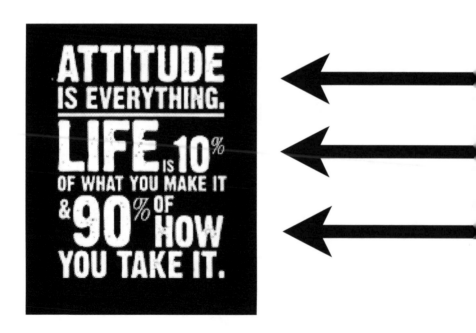

My mom would always say, "It's just nice to be nice," and that truth I hold as age-old wisdom. Life just happens, and we have to learn how to separate the negative response so that it doesn't affect our work. So if your co-workers are less than pleasant or if clients are running late back-to-back, remember to always press forward and continue to be professional despite the circumstance. With every interaction, you are representing your personal brand first.

5. Pay attention to the details

If you don't pay attention to the details, rest assured that your customers will. My high school coach would say, "Do the small things that matter." Paying attention to the smallest of details is a bit of a learned trait but will set you apart from the competition.

One way my salon differs from the average barbershop is that we offer squeaky-clean restrooms. It may not sound like much, but you would be surprised at how many times clients applaud that single differentiator. Maintaining a spotless restroom really stands out in a sea of less-than-tidy alternatives.

With so much shear talent in the beauty and style industry, little things like being timely, operating with integrity, being consistent, putting the customer first, and going the extra mile with no expectation, makes a huge difference. Clients don't ever have to question your professionalism because it speaks for itself. Again, do the small things first . . . and watch your business gain big rewards.

What are your differentiators? What makes you unique or different from the next hairstylist, barber, makeup artist, nail tech?

| My Core Differentiators | Areas of Improvement |
| --- | --- |
|  |  |
|  |  |
|  |  |
|  |  |

## Talent alone is not enough

Many don't know or won't admit it, but most stylist and barbers never make it in this industry due to their **lack of professionalism**. Well, let me be clear . . . I want to underscore that talent alone is not enough to sustain longevity. You can be good at what you do and make a decent living, but you will not become as great as you could be. Here's another way to look at it: Have you ever taken the time to distinguish the difference between the good and great stylists? If you have, you'll notice that there is in fact a sizable difference, and it shows in client retention, professional passion, and overall success in this industry. Having great talent without employing the art of professionalism is like having a tire with no air in it. It won't get you to your destination.

*Take the necessary steps today to go from good to great tomorrow.*

## There is no shortcut to success

I've learned over the years that there are some guiding principles to operating a successful business. In order to establish a winning work environment, you have to create a unique culture, know what type of team members to hire (and which to fire), and identify your target clientele. This I know for certain because truthfully, I have clients that have been with me for over 15 years. It is a testament to their belief in me—both of my talent and my level of professionalism. My clients know that when it comes to managing a successful salon and providing a superb customer experience, I don't take shortcuts.

## *You have to trust the process.*

Surround yourself with positive supporters

Find a mentor who is willing to help guide and direct you in the beginning, as it is a necessary requirement to develop great habits from day one. **Study those before you** who are successful and who have done well for themselves. Seek out mentors who are revered as business leaders, innovators of new ideas, or business processes. Their wisdom for the art and practice will be a necessary ingredient in your future growth and success.

Respect: Give to get it

Point blank, you have to earn it. Customers respect you and your business when they see that you respect them and yourself. How you manage your life and time directly correlates to how you will treat your customers. Remember this truth: *You will attract the type of clientele based on your level of professionalism.* So always check the temperature of your life to see if you are building a business that reflects your definition of success. It is never too late to give and earn respect.

## Being positive in a negative situation is not naive. It's leadership

I can't stress enough how important positive thinking is to your overall attainment of goals. It may seem fluffy or frivolous, but when you think positively, your circumstances do not adversely affect your disposition as much as they do when you think negatively. And when you start to understand that your attitude is within your own control, you'll uncover the key to a more successful life. So leave negative energy outside the salon or business because this type of energy could create turnover with employees and customers. Not only will it hurt you, but most importantly it will hurt your business and hinder your prospective growth. In the new age of social media (along with old-school word of mouth), having negative reviews written about your service will damage your business reputation in the long run. Be respectful of customers at all times, but never apologize for being passionate, professional, or operating with ethics.

## *The only person you're competing with is . . . you.*

For anyone who aspires to be a business owner in this industry, set up standards from day one. As you build your foundation, be patient, because it will certainly pay off in the end. When—not *if*— times get challenging, remember that you are establishing professional boundaries to protect the customer but also to provide a great work environment for yourself. Be sure to exercise patience during the team building process because attracting like-minded individuals is no easy feat. Great team members are like eagles: they are equal parts rare yet amazing. Do you recall the movie, *Field of Dreams* with Kevin Costner? Remember that small voice that kept saying, "Build it . . . they will come"? Well, no truer statement can be made. When a small business is not run with a professional spirit, the business will not survive long-term.

# NOTES

# NOTES

POINT #3

## *Be Your Best Brand.*

Be a yardstick of quality. Some people aren't used to an environment where excellence is expected.

Steve Jobs

The American Marketing Association (AMA) defines a brand as a "name, term, sign, symbol or design, or a combination of them intended to identify the goods and services of one seller or group of sellers and to differentiate them from those of other sellers."

Therefore it makes sense to understand that branding is not about getting your target market to choose you over the competition, but it is about getting your prospects to see you as the one that provides the best solution to their problem.

## *You attract who you are!*

<u>The value of branding</u>

Branding is one of the most important assets to understand and develop when you're first starting out. Essentially *your* name and reputation are the brand—whether you are working as a DBA ("doing business as") employee/ contractor, or you have your own salon or barber shop.

According to a 2011 report by American Profile, there were 220,000 barbers in the U.S., 41,340 barbershops, and 210,000 beauty salons—all amassing **$20 billion+** in annual revenue. With so many stylists employed in the beauty industry, how do you stay relevant and create a trustworthy track record? The answer: You have to become

**and remain** a great brand. But building a brand takes time and patience, consistency and practice. One of the main reasons beginners and new graduates fail to follow the branding rule of thumb is because of their eagerness to make money first. Don't make that same mistake. You have to trust the process.

## *Remember that it's OK to be different.*

<u>You are your brand</u>

As you start to think through the elements of your personal brand, remember that it beings and ends with you. Consider this example: You just received your state license, found a salon in which to work, and today is your first day on the job. The ultimate goal is to start building a strong clientele and/or following, correct?

Understand, this is not an overnight process by any means; trial and error are definitely part of the process. Your accomplishments as a student in school matter not in the real world in some cases, because when you were in school, the customers knew that they were entering an institution where the services were performed by students. If anything, your work product while in school served as a confidence booster. Nine times out of ten, you will *not* develop a long-term clientele from school after you graduate. But don't worry . . . look at that season as a time of preparation. These points I'm sharing with you are to help you push through and toward your brighter future. It is very easy to get caught up in developing your skills and talent and yet overlook your overall brand.

The most successful business professionals are memorable because they've been able to create a meaningful brand persona. Remember that **when your brand is effective, word-of-mouth advertising becomes your number one**

**asset** . . . this I promise. If you recall, I mentioned that talent alone is not enough. One negative review posted on social media or spread via word-of-mouth will rob you of potential customers and a great future in this industry. I can't promise that every day will be roses as you start to build and mature your brand, but I will say that having a plan and building your foundation from these methods will help guide you in the right direction.

At the end of the day, be the best *you* you can be.

# NOTES

# NOTES

POINT #4

## *Be Smart About Money.*

# Don't *tell* me what you value. Show me your budget and I'll tell you what you value.

Joe Biden

Yes, I have made more budget spreadsheets than I can count. And yes, it takes sacrifice and diligence to become fiscally responsible. The amount of time and effort it takes to build your business, create your brand, and set standards for your clients and you, is equal parts energy and patience as you learn how to manage your finances well. You may not want to hear it, but you *have* to separate your money in order to create a lifestyle that also supports your business. So where do you begin?

For starters, give every dollar a name. Keeping track of every dollar can be annoying if it's not something you are used to doing, but it helps to start early and build discipline into your daily routine. This practice of budgeting was very hard for me at first. However, when I started to list out everything I spent money on, I realized how much money I was wasting. It was shocking to believe that I was throwing it all away on frivolous things!

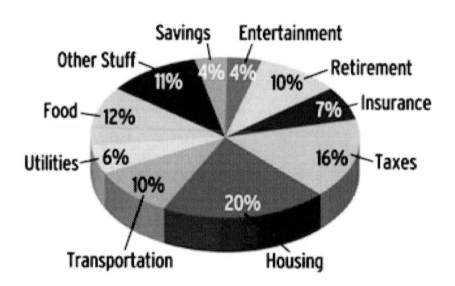

Second, save something . . . anything. When I began to make more and more money it became easier to save, but it also meant I had just as much more to waste. So I began to challenge myself to save—and the more I saved, the more I wanted to save. I ended up saving thousands of dollars, eventually funding my own salon with zero loans. If you feel like I did in the beginning and think that savings is something you'll do "later," put down this book and open up a savings account NOW. A good rule of thumb to start is to live off 80% of what you make, give 10%, and save the rest. You'll be amazed at how much you can amass by just exercising a little self-control.

### *Tye's Proven Budget Formula, the 80/10/10 Rule:*
## *Spend <u>80%</u>, Give <u>10%</u>, and Save <u>10%</u>*

When I first started my salon 15 years ago, I thought it was as simple as saving some money, finding retail space, buying the necessary equipment and tools, and building out more stations for other potential stylists, barbers, nail techs, etc. My goodness, was I wrong . . . so wrong. After checking those items off my list, never did I realize that it was just the framework. I knew absolutely nothing about budgeting for a business, separating my personal expenditures from business expenses, or about managing the overhead involved. It was a rude awakening for me. I almost called it quits after the first 6 months, and the next two years were even more of a struggle. After hiring an amazing accountant and realizing that my life would change dramatically because of the financial sacrifices I would have to make, the next three-five years were a blur. I was forced to change my mindset, the way I lived, and my money habits.

*I almost called it quits after the first 6 months, and the next 2 years were even more of a struggle.*

Truth be told, understanding money and budgeting takes skill, practice and discipline, but mostly discipline. My life today and how I see money is not even the same as it was

15 years ago. It's definitely changed for the good, but I had to really make it a habit. Learning how to budget for both my business and personal expenses was a difficult process. I went from renting a booth one day and bringing home all of my money, to being a business owner and writing myself a check for one-third of what I used to make. And the rest was reserved for overhead to keep my business going.

*I went from renting a booth and bringing home all of my money to being a business owner and writing myself a check for 1/3 of what I used to make.*

If you have a business or aspire to start your own business of any kind, know that overhead expenses are inevitable. These expenses are necessary and create potential growth. For example, you may have a monthly lease, product inventory, electrical, gas, and water bills to pay. How are you going to manage a thriving business if you don't even set budgets in your personal life? Take it from me: It's impossible to succeed without having a budget mindset. That's like buying a car and expecting it to run without gasoline. At the end of the day, you have to be fiscally responsible.

Take the time to think, plan ahead, and be aware of the costs needed to develop a successful business. Remember that not all the money you bring in is your money.

## *At the end of the day, you have to be fiscally responsible.*

Budgeting is a skill all its own, and why they do not make money management a required course for every graduating high schooler baffles me. I have worked with so many people in this industry, each with their own perspective on money, and I've learned that those who established a budget early on are those who are still running successful businesses today. Early in my career I had co-workers who would work a few hours and then leave for the day with what they made *that day* to go shopping. How silly and irresponsible it is to settle for a few dollars that you blow away in a matter of minutes! Sad to say, those same folks who settled for mediocrity then are now forced to work multiple jobs just to make ends meet today.

Third, there is such a thing called overhead. I mentioned overhead a few paragraphs back but want to stress its importance. Overhead is all the bills and other financial responsibilities that are required to keep your business operating. For example, you can almost always count on having marketing expenses (business cards, Website, promotions, etc.), cost for your styling tools and products, merchant accounts, electricity, cable, lease/rent, and cleaning services. All these things have to be taken into consideration before you waste a dime. So again, if you don't budget or learn to budget, you will eventually fail to maintain and grow your business productively. I'd hate to see you become part of the 20% of beauty school graduates who bow out after five short years. Don't be a statistic.

Instead, take a few moments now and answer these questions:

1. How much do I want to make? In a month, in a quarter, in a year?

_____

_____

2. How many clients do I need to service in order to generate that much revenue?

_____

3. How will I identify those clients? Where do I look?

_____

4. How can I generate more revenue from each client? What value-add can I provide?

_____

_____

## *Telling your money what to do will make it work harder.*

For a simple starter guide to budgeting, download Dave Ramsey's Guide to Budgeting: http://tinyurl.com/brjlt6u.

I highly recommend any of his resources.

# NOTES

# NOTES

## Point #5
### *Be Consistent.*

# Consistency is better than rare moments of greatness.

Author unknown

As long as I've been in business, I've never missed a day of work without first taking care of my clients. Now I don't say that to pat myself on the back; I make that statement to share a bit of knowledge that I've learned from firsthand experience. If you've ever heard the saying, "Showing up is half the battle," then you understand that your consistent presence will inevitably produce results. By simply *being there*, your business will thrive and your clients will appreciate your respect for the business.

*Consistency is very important to building your career. It will ultimately determine your longevity or demise.*

<u>Being consistent will set you apart from your competitors</u>

When I first set out to open my own salon, I wanted to do things differently—not just from a services point of view but also from an operations perspective. One of the best practices I implemented that I still carry out today is setting appointments: from Tuesday through Friday, my calendar is slotted with scheduled client sessions. This exercise not only helps keep my regular clients on a consistent cadence, but it also helps me maintain regularity in my day-to-day operations. And clients notice this sort of nuance, which ultimately sets me apart from the competition.

However, it didn't start out that way; I had to patiently build my clientele day-by-day in order to get to that point in my career. And even in my naivete as a business owner, I knew that doing the little things every day would be vital to my becoming successful. Remember that building takes time, but consistency puts you on the right path to make a great name for yourself.

When you have developed the character to become consistent, it is one of the best compliments a client can give you because it speaks volumes to who you are as an individual. Oftentimes it's loaded with other compliments like, "You are really good at your craft" or "No one can ever duplicate your work," or better yet, "I've never looked this good!" All of these statements are a compliment to your talent and hard work. But did you know that timeliness is just as significant?

When you are a timely individual, you demonstrate that you care about your clients' time as well as your own and that you conduct your business in a professional manner **on a regular basis**. Basically, being consistent with your time can either make or break you, because it is just as important as the need to be professional.

## *Consistency is better than rare moments of greatness.*

Settling down doesn't meant you have to settle

I've witnessed countless stylists hop from salon to salon and barbershop to barbershop. When I counsel young stylists, I advise them to exercise their options and find what works best for them. For some, that could be identifying an environment that they can call home for an extended period of time. Any sign of instability will not only hurt your business but will also damage your brand and most of all, your integrity with both prospective and current clients. Be mindful of where you choose to operate your business, as clients will judge you (either fairly or unfairly) by your surroundings. Know that professionalism and consistency go hand and hand; one without the other is detrimental to your long-term success.

## Education doesn't end when you graduate

On the contrary: continuing education is a must while you are building up a clientele base. When you are/were in school, you were taught basic foundational skills. Once you get out and step into the real world, you have to keep the process of learning going because there are always new ways of styling, innovative service ideas, changing trends, and so on. So stay in the know and at the pivotal point of change. The basics won't change, but with continued education classes you will stay ahead of the curve. By attending classes, you'll gain a larger network of like-minded peers in the industry as well.

## Have faith in your abilities

This is "old school" knowledge but something that most people quickly forget when in the throes of building a business: Believe in yourself from day one and always learn from your mistakes. It will become the most positive aspect in your journey toward success. I have made so many mistakes that have become the biggest assets in my life. Remember that being mentored by failure is not necessarily a bad thing!

## Don't be afraid to go the extra mile

There are really no short cuts to success, so I encourage you to learn all you can, because you will need that information as you progress along your career path. Take advantage of all the information you receive. Treat people like you want to be treated and do not ever waver from that statute.

I've seen too many of my peers and co-workers fail in this industry—very talented individuals who oozed success from the start but lacked that extra something that wouldn't allow them to do the little things that really matter. When I say *little things*, I mean things like: being considerate of clients' time, providing feedback about customer concerns, offering complimentary consultations, and being able to engage in mature conversation.

Do not limit yourself to one skill set; learn as much as you can on your journey because it will open up other areas of opportunity that will create additional income for you and your family. Always go that extra mile . . . it will work in your favor every time.

# NOTES

# NOTES

## Bonus Material

It is your Work in life that is the ultimate seduction.

Pablo Picasso

*This section is part self-help guide, part management tutorial.*

I host many seminars, speaking engagements, and one-on-ones with professionals in a variety of industries who desire more success. As a small business owner and mentor to individuals who want to be start their own business, I try to provide truth and hope, because if there is one thing I have learned, it's that starting something is easy but the real work comes after you start.

I'll never forget my own experience when I opened the doors of my salon more than fourteen years ago. (I've been in this industry over two decades now.) After managing a salon for six years, I decided to go it alone and open my own business, thinking that it couldn't possibly be that difficult. I had no idea what I was getting myself into! After spending months searching for a suitable location, I wiped out all of my savings to purchase an existing salon business. Three months later, I called my mother for some encouragement because I had started to second guess myself. What had I gotten myself into?! Bills were coming at me left and right, the old guard wasn't responding to the culture I was trying to create, and this thing called a profit and loss statement was foreign to me. But I **kept showing up and doing the little things that matter.** The experience I gained from that season has earned me priceless knowledge that college probably could not have afforded me.

*If you do all the small things right,*

*BIG THINGS can happen.*

## You have to love what you do

One of the greatest difficulties in being an entrepreneur and having your own business is setting the foundation and creating an enviable culture. Foundation is the idea, an underlying basis and principle for something. Culture is having distinct values, respect and ideologies that have been created for the team members and customers alike. Most salons and barbershops are pretty basic; however some have added twists here and there for surface exterior. But if there isn't a major difference that sets you apart from the rest, you will just blend in with the others. At the end of the day, your **professionalism**, the **quality of work**, and the **environment for your customers** are what will allow you to stand out amongst the competition.

Lastly, we really need to think about the customer more so than ourselves, because they help to keep the lights on . . . literally. I *chose* this career. It didn't choose me. Twenty years later, I enjoy it more today than I did when I first started. The beauty and style industry has taken me places I never could have imagined and afforded me an unbelievable lifestyle. My hope is that you, too, experience success according to your own definition. Just remember that "it is your work in life that is the *ultimate* seduction."

## *It is your Work in life that is the* ultimate *seduction.*

# NOTES

# NOTES

# EPILOGUE
## *Frequently Asked Questions*

*Congratulations!* You've just completed in days what it took me twenty years to master. Now that you know success in this industry is not about the hair, what will you start to do differently today? Right now? Really take the five points I've shared with you to heart. Start where you are and take baby steps. But **start now** because consistency, discipline, and persistence will win out every time. Remember: Your go-forward success depends on your *professionalism*, <u>not</u> your skill set.

Here are a few Frequently Asked Questions that new stylists ask me. Hopefully the responses will encourage you and provide hope along the way.

**What is an entrepreneur?**

*Wikipedia says that an entrepreneur is seen commonly as a business leader, innovator of new ideas, and business processes.*

*The Webster Dictionary defines it as a person who organizes, operates, and assumes risk of a business venture.*

## *Entrepreneurship: the act and art of being an entrepreneur.*

**Is there one piece of advice I should heed before starting my own business?**

*Laying down the proper foundation is very important to starting any business: Remember . . . nothing will last if the foundation on which it is built is not stable and consistent.*

Stability is everything. Be it emotional or physical. You need a solid ground to build anything on.

Author unknown

**What types of things should I consider before stepping out on my own?**

*1. You have to be a risk taker.*

*2. You should be passionate about what you want to do.*

*3. Give heed/meditate on the steps you need to take.*

*4. Know your financial makeup. Are you financially capable to step out on your own?*

*5. Have a plan to execute!*

*6. Make sure you keep valued supporters and mentors around you for the necessary push, because the entire process can be overwhelming at times.*

*7. Come up with your own definition of success.*

**Once I get my business or company started, what sort of questions do I need to answer before the real work begins?**

- *Are you ready to work harder than you ever have?*

- *Are you prepared to work long hours . . . going in early and staying extra late?*

- *Can you/will you budget every penny you spend?*

- *Would you be able to hire and fire employees?*

- *Are you OK with having no vacations for awhile?*

- *Are you ready to lose time being with family and friends?*

- *Do I have a network of supporters who will encourage me unconditionally? Who are my accountability partners?*

- *How will I pick myself up and get back on track when I experience a patch of really tough days?*

**In your opinion, what is required to see a new business flourish?**

*Sacrifice and determination*

# You've got what it takes. But it will take everything you've got.

**How do you set the tone for a creative culture that will keep contractors and customers coming back for more?**

*I've had the same team members since I first opened my salon. One thing I did at the beginning was to make sure there were guidelines for running the business for the purpose of creating structure.*

*Every entrepreneur-business owner must create a company culture that will set the tone for:*

- *how he/she wants to be represented*

- *creating a particular work environment*

- *knowing what type of team members to hire*

- *the type of clientele you would like to market to*

TYE CALDWELL

**How do you recommend I market my brand-new business?**

*Firstly, tell everyone you know that you're open for business! Anyone is a potential client: neighbors, friends, your child's teachers, the guy who works out at the gym. It is a requirement that you market your business in order to reach potential customers. If you're not talking about it, no one else is. Secondly, test advertise in local chamber of commerce mailings and invest in SEM (search engine marketing) to help drive leads. There is no better marketing than word of mouth, so be sure to provide exceptional service. Remember that what is said about your business online—either positive or negative—will reflect on the business and mostly the business owner.*

## *In the beginning, if you're not talking about your business, no one else will.*

*Whether by word of mouth or social media, remember, the service you provide and your quality of work will determine the consistency of the repeat business and the overall success of your business. There are other marketing tools and strategies you can use to for your business to be visible, however it can be very costly. Do your research and determine what types of promotions and budget will work for you.*

**Should I use social media to market my business?**

*Absolutely! Take advantage of the freemium platforms like Twitter, Instagram, YouTube, Facebook, Periscope, and Yelp. Showcase your work. Potential clients like to see and hear testimonials from happy customers.*

**Any other advice you would give to first-time entrepreneurs?**

*Jump and grow your wings on the way down! And when you make it, PAY. IT. FORWARD.*

# NOTES

# NOTES

# *Afterword*

As I have seen over my 20 years of studying leadership and leading large groups of individuals, if you are intentional about focusing on the right things and being patient, you will see success come to fruition. That's the message we've read over and over again throughout the pages of *Mentored by Failure*. If you focus on Tye's five key points, you are capable of accomplishing anything. Though this book is based on achievement in the beauty and style industry, the points shared can be used to create success in any field and in any area of your life.

*Mentored by Failure* highlights this point to its fullest, and the examples that Tye sets forth in using his failures to help accomplish his goals are encouraging. What a unique, well-timed, and culturally-appropriate book we can use to drive individuals to success!

In a world where many allow their dreams and goals to be thwarted by past missteps, *Mentored by Failure* shows that if we allow God to work, He can use our past failures to guide us towards a bright future. As Tye wields his personal journey to pull out five main points that are the basis to a long and successful career, I am certain that many will be able to use his expert advice as a catalyst to push them closer to success.

As the reader digests each chapter—but also looks beyond the words—we see how small, consistent changes make a world of difference as we inch towards our goals. I encourage everyone to go forth and "Be Focused," "Be Professional," "Be Your Best Brand," "Be Smart About Money," and "Be Consistent" as you dream big. On the journey, be sure to keep this book close to you so it can be used when you need a refresher or words of wisdom to share.

Dr. Conway Edwards
www.visitonecc.com

You're the only one who can make
the difference. Whatever your dream is,
go for it.

Earvin "Magic" Johnson

## *About the Author*

Tye Caldwell, Owner of Salon74 by Tye and Founder of R.I.S.E. Professional Training & Coaching, is a community leader and salon entrepreneur. His classic approach to professionalism and small business management has earned him a diligent following, and his expertise in helping others achieve their "best self" is unmatched.

Tye has an innate ability to help others uncover and maximize their full potential and has spent the last decade meeting market demand as a coach and consultant. Through R.I.S.E. Professional Training & Coaching, Mr. Caldwell's portfolio of work has quickly expanded from single parents and disadvantaged youth to business leaders and corporate executives.

Mr. Tyrone Caldwell has spent the last several years sharing his wisdom and real-world experience with the next generation of salon owners and beauty school graduates. As they embark upon their road to success, Mr. Caldwell "pays it forward" by coaching cosmetologists and offering his 20+ years of industry knowledge as a proven roadmap.

Tye serves on the Advisory Board of the Ogle School of Cosmetology & Esthetics, as a Board member of Galaxy Counseling Center (a local not-for-profit), and is a frequent guest speaker at Texas Barber College & Hairstyling School.

His flagship salon, Salon74 by Tye, was awarded the 2015 "Reader's Choice Award" and named the "Best of Plano" Beauty Salon in 2014. Mr. Caldwell's work has been featured on Channel 4 KDFW and Channel 8 WFAA, and he has been honored by local non-profits such as Big Brothers Big Sisters, The Potter's House Church in Dallas, Frisco ISD, and numerous ministries for his unremitting service to the community. When he's not pouring into the lives of others, Mr. Caldwell enjoys international travel, reading, and spending time with his wife and son.

Connect with him on Twitter @salon74bytye, on Instagram @salon74bytye, or via email at tye@salon74bytye.com.

It's not good to have only one sense. Use *all* your senses when it comes to life. Be well-rounded.

Houston Caldwell, Sr. (Dad)

Printed in the United States of America